For Your Garden

ROSE GARDENS

For Your Garden

ROSE GARDENS

WARREN SCHULTZ

FRIEDMAN/FAIRFAX
PUBLISHERS

A FRIEDMAN/FAIRFAX BOOK

Library of Congress Cataloging-in-Publication data available upon request.

ISBN 1-56799-398-2

Editor: Susan Lauzau
Art Director: Lynne Yeamans
Layout: Maria Mann
Photography Editor: Wendy Missan

Color separations by Fine Arts Repro House Co., Ltd.
Printed in China by Leefung-Asco Printers Ltd.

For bulk purchases and special sales, please contact:
Friedman/Fairfax Publishers
Attention: Sales Department
15 West 26th Street
New York, New York 10010
212/685-6610   FAX 212/685-1307

Visit the Friedman/Fairfax Website:
http://www.webcom.com/friedman/

Table of Contents

INTRODUCTION

*F*or its lore, mystique, and romance, the rose stands alone. *Planting a rose introduces its rich heritage to your landscape, and we recall its storied past every time we glimpse its vibrant beauty or inhale its delicate fragrance. Countless poems have been written about the rose; wars have been fought over it; and it's been an ingredient in the formulas of medieval alchemists. More than any other flower we can plant, the rose represents love and affection. It truly embodies the perfection of nature.*

With its flawless flower, its tantalizing fragrance, and its classic form, a rose can transform a garden. Whether alone in a long formal bed, mixed with perennials in a border, or climbing a porch, roses always seem to fit your landscape—and your desires.

Roses freely contribute their majesty to a garden. All eyes are drawn to them when they are in bloom. But they are capable of surprising, too. They can be modest like the simple, humble blooms of New England shining roses (Rosa nitida). They can be as informal as the glossy foliage and bright hips of rugosa roses (Rosa rugosa). Or they can display the exuberance of wild rambling roses. However you choose to use them, roses are sure to serve as the crowning touch in your garden.

ABOVE: It's easy to get lost in the perfect bloom of a rose. Whether the flowers are single and simplicity itself or double and full—like those of this floribunda, 'Margaret Merril'—rose blossoms, pure and fragrant, add enchantment to any garden scene.

OPPOSITE: Roses bring a feeling of luxury to the landscape. Many rose classes offer a profusion of blooms on thick, full bushes that add drama to a vast landscape or even to just the corner of a bed. Here, the shrub rose 'Constance Spry' covers itself with fragrant pink blooms in high summer.

ABOVE: For all their majesty, roses fit in gracefully with other flowering and foliage plants, serving here as an exclamation point in a border of herbaceous perennials. The white blooms of the shrub rose 'Nevada' appear in midsummer and continue to rebloom until autumn.

LEFT: A rosebush is the ultimate enticement. The pure pink blooms of the gallica rose 'Versicolor' anchor a seating area and make it even more inviting. Gallica roses, first grown by the Romans, exude a delicious fragrance that's difficult to resist.

ABOVE: Asked to imagine a single rose, most of us would picture the delicately folded blossom of a hybrid tea. In truth, hybrid teas are fairly recent introductions to the world of roses. But every garden should have at least one, to add "rose-ness" to the landscape and elegance to the home as a cut flower.

RIGHT: There are so many classes and cultivars of roses, and the plants and blooms occur in such an assortment of forms and hues, that it's easy to find an ideal cultivar for any type of surroundings. This shrub rose seems perfectly at home adorning the porch of a rustic cottage.

ABOVE: Like a living tapestry, the climbing rose 'Constance Spry' hangs over a brick wall. Its intoxicating scent drifts over a classic white bench, creating a nearly irresistible resting spot.

OPPOSITE: Hundreds of years of breeding have given birth to increasingly complex roses, but the plant's ancient roots have not been forgotten. A species rose such as *Rosa glauca* is a welcome addition to the landscape for its simple, starlike flower and striking, blue-gray foliage.

ABOVE: Roses are so commanding that all it takes is a single bloom to lift the landscape out of the ordinary. The exquisitely striped pink-and-white floribunda 'Peppermint Twist' offers a scintillating splash of color.

LEFT: Something unusual happened in the breeding of hybrid teas. Plants occasionally threw up sports—mutant plants with new characteristics. Such a sport was the origin of the climbing rose, which allows us to enjoy the prolific blooms of the hybrid teas in vertical spaces.

ABOVE: The rediscovery of antique roses makes one wonder why they were ever neglected. Old roses, such as this 'Rosa Mundi', contribute a feeling of timelessness to the formal garden.

ABOVE: Sometimes roses are most appreciated when they are allowed to dominate, with just a bit of help from a supporting cast. The lanky growth of Bourbon roses can be complemented with an underplanting of simple flowers such as pansies.

LEFT: As if the fantastic blooms, enchanting fragrance, regal foliage, and stunning form of roses were not enough, many offer an autumn show of glossy hips. This fruit—popular in teas, jams, and jellies—endures to decorate the winter landscape.

ABOVE: Roses rise to the occasion in this formal island bed. Climbing varieties, such as 'Madame Caroline Testout', will readily clamber up a support, adding height and color to the garden.

ABOVE: Fairy tales and storybooks come to mind as the visitor approaches this scene. The climbing rose, intertwined with white-flowering clematis, is the final magical touch.

ABOVE: Roses can serve as a centerpiece or they can contribute their enchantment from afar. A house in the distance is honored by the 'Morning Jewel' rose that frames a view of it.

ABOVE: At home in the cottage garden, the formal border, or the wild landscape, roses are never too refined to fit into a garden. 'Scarlet Fire', a recently introduced shrub rose, manages to combine elegance with a casual air.

ABOVE: Floating like a cloud, the crystalline blooms of 'Iceberg' roses draw the eye toward the focal point of the garden, a magnificent urn filled with geraniums. While not technically the central players in this lush garden, the roses serve as a lovely frame for the picture.

OPPOSITE: The wise gardener considers form and color when combining roses with other plants. These tall, spiky delphiniums are emphasized by the cascade of pale roses in the background.

Chapter One

SOCIABLE CLIMBERS

*I*t almost seems too much to ask: a cascade of flawless flowers in intricate forms and bright colors spilling over a fence or climbing up a wall, releasing their alluring scent into the evening air. But climbing roses bring that dream within reach of every gardener.

Roses are at their most dramatic when they're growing up and over a support. Climbing and rambling roses evoke the feeling of antiquity as they scale an arbor, clamber over a fence, or cover a brick building.

In these plants you can sense the wild nature of early roses. They carry a sense of abandon into the garden as vigorous canes lift the flowers to eye level and beyond, displaying the glorious flowers and allowing their scent to tumble on the wind.

Another benefit of climbing roses: these exuberant plants grow fast, filling a garden with sheer vitality. And they do it without complaint. All that's required is an annual pruning to remove old and damaged canes, and winter protection in cold areas.

OPPOSITE: Though roses have no tendrils to pull themselves up a brick wall, a thin wire provides enough support. The wire seems to disappear behind the shiny green foliage and bright blooms of a climbing rose such as 'Celine Forrestier'.

RIGHT: A landscape can be created with climbing roses as the focal point. Two climbing roses, 'Helen Knight' and 'Madame Alfred Carriere', meet above a leaded glass window. A bed of pale yellow irises in the foreground adds the dimension of contrasting flower form to the scene.

ABOVE: What goes up can also come down. Climbing roses appear most roman-
tic when they are allowed to hang and trail gracefully. Here, 'Alister Stella Grey'
lends atmosphere to a latticed garden bench.

OPPOSITE: Climbing roses are often at their best when seen from below. Framed
by a bright blue sky, the pale pink climber 'New Dawn' comes alive. Just two of
these vigorous plants will quickly cover a trellis.

ABOVE: A 'Queen of Denmark' rose floats whimsically over a bench. Just a single plant clambering up an arbor softens the hard edges of the landscape and showers the sitting area with its sweet scent.

LEFT: Roses add grace and grandeur to any garden scene. As 'Lady Hillingdon' scrambles over an arched gate, it refreshes the landscape. Climbing roses are the focal point of this scene, rising above the clipped box in an urn and hostas in the distance.

ABOVE: Roses are not solitary creatures. They'll happily combine with many other forms of garden flowers and foliage. Here, the roses 'Minnehaha' and 'Aloha' prove perfect companions for clematis and campanula.

LEFT: Roses can own a landscape. An entire pergola in this English garden is given over to 'Rambling Rector' rose, adding an aura of lushness to the well-manicured lawn.

ABOVE: All roses offer a rainbow of colors, but the varied class of climbing and rambling roses offers a wide selection of foliage and flower forms as well. 'American Pillar', for instance, is covered with clusters of tiny flowers.

ABOVE: By nature, climbing and rambling roses invite admiration from a distance. But step in for a closer look at *Rosa* 'Verschuren', the Lambook rose—each flower inspires awe with its delicate, ruffled bloom.

RIGHT: 'Paul's Scarlet' covers a pergola with rich red blooms in midsummer. Though it blossoms only once a season, its semidouble bloom blankets the foliage. This variety also makes a fine shrub rose if pruned regularly.

ABOVE: No matter what fills the surrounding garden, a rose pergola always serves as the ultimate destination. It draws us to bask in the color and scent of the flowers that drape it. This stately wood and brick pergola is decked with masses of 'Aloha', 'Sanders White', and 'Compassion'.

ABOVE: A rustic pergola serves as a perfect support for a collection of climbing roses. It lifts the striking blooms of 'Bleu Magenta'—one of the more unusual climbers—above the surrounding perennials. Here, the bluish red rose is flanked by companion climbers 'Wedding Day' and 'Botany Bay'.

LEFT: Climbing roses do have one shortcoming—some have a short bloom time. But there's an easy and elegant fix: fill in the blanks with a companionable climber like this large-flowered purple clematis.

29

ABOVE: Though it is a tender plant and requires some pampering, yellow Lady Banks' rose (*Rosa banksiae* var. *lutea*) is well worth the trouble. Its small flowers cover the vine with a dazzling display of blooms in early spring.

OPPOSITE: Climbing roses almost always represent a riot of disorganized bloom and foliage. Here, a border of well-tended lavender along a stone path balances the exuberant blooms with order and definition.

ABOVE: Rambling roses offer even more vigorous growth than their cousins, the climbers. Ramblers have more flexible canes, a trait that allows the plants to be used as groundcovers. Or, like this 'Tausendschon', ramblers may be trained to scramble over a wall.

ABOVE: Sometimes even roses that are not classed as climbers can be persuaded to adopt a rambling habit. 'The Fairy' is an exceedingly vigorous shrub rose that shines when it is left to scurry over a split rail fence. As a bonus, it's hardier than most climbers.

OPPOSITE: Is there anything in the world of horticulture that says "welcome" better than climbing roses adorning a door? A 'Penelope' rose lends an inviting softness to this somewhat austere dooryard.

Chapter Two

THE REST OF THE ROSES

hat's in a name? Plenty. A rose by any other name might smell as sweet, but when it comes to planning and planting the landscape, it helps to understand the nomenclature of roses. That might seem an impossible task to the beginner. There are scores of different classes of roses, from the ancient Rosa chinensis, or China roses, to the modern shrub roses. Over centuries of breeding the lines have blurred until even experienced rosarians argue over them.

In general, though, each class has its own characteristics and requirements. A basic familiarity with these classes and the cultivars within them can help you choose the right roses for your situation.

In time you can learn the subtleties of the rose, but what's most important is to choose a look you like, whether it's the simple single bloom of a wild rose or the elaborate swirl of a hybrid tea. First choose the rose that takes your breath away—the one that seems to have been bred for your garden and your sensibility—and then take the time to learn about it.

ABOVE: Modern roses, sometimes called modern crosses, combine the best of the old and the new, blurring the distinctions between the lines. The English rose is a new category. Its most famous breeder is David Austin, and a type has been named after him. David Austin roses are known for their hardiness, fragrance, and double flowers in pastel hues. 'Graham Thomas', the first yellow English rose, was one of Austin's creations.

OPPOSITE: Shrub roses encompass many classes, both old and new. All of them are welcome in the garden for their robust habit, and flowers may be once- or repeat-blooming. 'Pink Meidiland' has striking pink blossoms with white eyes, and blooms in both spring and autumn. This hardy and disease-resistant rose grows rapidly, topping off at four feet (1.2m).

ABOVE: A specialized form of the modern shrub rose, the hybrid musk is a wonder. The plant is rangy and rambling, best when combined with other plants in a mixed bed or border, but the flowers are refined. Blooming in delicate pastel shades, blossoms usually turn white as they fade. 'Buff Beauty' is a prolific repeat-bloomer that is constantly covered with roses in all stages of flowering.

ABOVE: When it comes to blooms, there's no rose that can surpasses the elegant, perfect, folded-petal form of the hybrid tea. And red 'Christian Dior' is the epitome of the hybrid tea rose.

OPPOSITE: Musk roses also come in a rambler form that makes a good addition to the informal cottage garden. 'Paul's Himalayan Musk Rambler' sports a pink blush on its glistening white blooms.

ABOVE: The multiflora rose, now naturalized throughout the United States, is native to China. Its origin gives a clue to its vigor and hardiness. As persistent as a weed—in fact it has been declared a weed in some areas—it produces abundant bright white blooms that are held in large, tight clusters.

ABOVE: Damask roses are among the most honored of old types. They first adorned the pleasure gardens of ancient Persia, and were later brought to Europe by the crusaders. 'Leda' is a very fragrant cultivar that it is winter hardy as well as virtually disease-free.

ABOVE: The multiflora species has been utilized as a parent for floribunda, polyantha, and musk roses, as well as for hybrid multifloras. 'Veilchenblau' is one of the more spectacular of the multiflora hybrids. It produces just a single flush of blooms in midseason, but the flowers cover this twelve-foot rambler (3.6m) with rich color, while exuding the scent of apples.

ABOVE: The Noisette class of roses was developed in the nineteenth century in South Carolina, and was named after their breeder, Philippe Noisette. They became a sensation for their repeat bloom and for their attractive clusters of clove-scented flowers. The Noisettes fell out of favor nearly one hundred years ago, but cultivars such as 'Crepuscule' are leading the class in a comeback.

ABOVE: Born of rambling parents, the polyanthas are tough and independent, requiring minimal care. They flower freely with little or no pruning. 'Ellen Poulsen' produces masses of clear pink blooms on a short bush.

ABOVE: 'Baronne Prevost' is a rose beyond reproach. Its refined, deeply scrolled blossoms, in shades of pale to deep pink, exude a rich, classic rose fragrance. And unlike its hybrid perpetual kin, the bush is vigorous and attractive.

LEFT: The origin of the miniature rose is shrouded in mystery, but there's no question about its utility. True miniatures, such as this creamy orange 'Chrissy', are scaled-down roses in bloom, leaf, and plant form. They're perfect for pots or window boxes, or as low border plants along a sunny path.

ABOVE: Growing a 'Caribbean' rose is like capturing the most spectacular sunset for your garden. The textured orange blooms adorn a strong bush, typical of its grandiflora class.

ABOVE: For those rosarians who like their flowers simple, 'Encore' is a perfect choice. This charming floribunda produces masses of blooms in a light pink blush.

ABOVE: The grandiflora is a relatively new class of roses, developed from floribunda stock in the 1950s. Roses in this family are characterized by clusters of flowers on towering bushes, though 'White Lightnin' is one of the smaller examples of the class.

ABOVE: Floribunda roses live up to their ambitious name. Derived from a fortuitous cross between ramblers and polyanthas, floribundas produce seemingly impossible masses of flowers. The bushes are also hardier and more disease resistant than those of hybrid teas. 'Golden Fleece' offers lush, bright yellow blooms.

ABOVE: The Bourbons seem to be almost perfect roses. Insistent repeat-bloomers, they flower prolifically through summer until the first frost. And what blooms! Complex, many-layered, and delicate, in shades of pink—like this 'Zephirine Drouhin'—the plants are vigorous, disease resistant, and winter hardy. They're wonderful along a walk, where their fragrance perfumes the air.

RIGHT: You'll find the rugosa rose growing wild along the seashore, as tough and vigorous as a weed. This rose's thick, hairy foliage and bright, single, fragrant blooms fit perfectly into the natural or casual garden. In fact it'll grow just about anywhere, dressing the garden with festive blooms in summer and colorful round hips in autumn.

ABOVE: The China rose, *Rosa chinensis*, is the parent of many of our modern roses, and has brought the enviable quality of repeat blooming to many cultivars. Though the blooms of many China roses are simple, almost dull compared with the complex flower forms other roses, the rich, pink blooms of *R. chinensis mutabilis* look like delicate butterflies at rest.

LEFT: There's been a boom in the breeding of modern roses, which has given rise to a whole new class, the David Austin roses. Named after their creator, the Austins are fine shrub roses, known for their hardy bushes, repeat blooms, and fragrant flowers. 'Prospero' is a fine example.

Chapter Three

ROSES AND THE COMPANY THEY KEEP

*W*e think of roses as the royalty of the garden. True enough, over centuries of cultivation, they've earned a singular position in the landscape. Roses are strong enough to stand alone in the garden. But, because many do not bloom all season, they lend themselves well to integration with other types of plants.

Fortunately, roses are happy to share the stage. They will make themselves at home in the formal border, and they'll mix with an understory of annuals or a background of shrubs. Climbing roses or ramblers can serve as an exciting background for any type of plant. The rose's versatility is among its most unappreciated qualities.

The range of bloom colors, too, makes the rose a gardener's dream. From pale peaches and pinks to cool yellows to fiery reds and oranges—and even a few blues—there's sure to be a rose that matches your garden's color scheme.

OPPOSITE: Climbing roses might look sparse against a brick wall or may appear bare when flowers fade, but the tall flower spikes of foxglove help to fill in any empty spaces.

RIGHT: A four-foot (1.2m)-tall 'Iceberg' rosebush serves as a focal point in this garden. Its glowing white blooms give the eye an area of focus between the trees in the background and the herbaceous perennials in the foreground. A bamboo plant helps to ease the transition in height.

ABOVE: The bare stems of the climbing 'Ferdinand de Lesseps' rose are hidden by exuberant stalks of *Penstemon digitalis* in this border garden. The airy white penstemon help to sustain the illusion that the roses are floating against the brick.

LEFT: Companion plants for a rose garden should be chosen with their blooming seasons in mind. Bright yellow lily-flowered tulips are a perfect complement to the early-blooming 'Hugonis' rose in the background. The sweet blue blossoms of forget-me-nots round out this garden picture.

OPPOSITE: In some plantings, roses are at their best when they're allowed to play a supporting role. A single 'Buff Beauty' bush at the edge of this bed offers a unifying color element to the delphinium and lysimachia.

ABOVE: Roses don't have to be aloof in the garden. Their majesty is evident even when surrounded by other plants. A 'Camaieux' rose peeks through the bright blooms of *Stachys macrantha* and red valerian.

LEFT: Tall, lanky roses such as the alba 'Queen of Denmark' are at their best when surrounded by lofty garden plants. Here, 'Pink Beauty' tiger lily, *Phlomis italica,* and wallflower lend their enthusiastic presence.

ABOVE: Companion plants don't have to conform to the standard set by roses in order to work well. These small potted violas and alyssums make perfect partners for 'Cecile Brunner'. The rose seems to be bending in a friendly gesture to greet the diminutive flowers.

ABOVE: A simple combination in a small bed can heighten the magical effect of roses. This modest planting features height and depth with lavender, orange lilies, and the spectacular hybrid tea rose 'Tanzenroh'.

ABOVE: Roses can serve as an elegant filler in a bed or border. 'Compte de Chambord' and 'Veilchenblau' close the gaps and soften the edges of a pergola that is surrounded by a planting of honeysuckle, delphiniums, and catmint.

RIGHT: Pay attention to the harmony of colors when planning a garden around roses. Complementary colors work best, as when 'Fritz Nobis', a light pink rose, grows alongside purple berberis.

ABOVE: A sprawling pearly rose serves admirably to hold together the divergent plants—including lilies and hostas—in this white garden. When viewed at night the white blooms will seem to shimmer and glow in the moonlight.

ABOVE: Maybe all roads lead to Rome, but in some gardens, all plants lead to the rose. Purple geraniums and *Acanthus spinosus* set the stage for the daring red of a 'Charles de Mills' rose.

ABOVE: Roses will welcome other climbers. A careful and well-considered combination adds luster to their presence. Here, the rose 'Zephirine Drouhin' shares a trellis with *Clematis niobe.*

ABOVE: An 'American Pillar' rose adds elegance and order to a riotous border, rising up above the campanula, hollyhocks, phlox, and other plants. Heavy paving stones come to the aid of the roses in keeping this garden on the straight and narrow.

RIGHT: Shrub roses can occasionally appear severe and formal, a habit that may make them seem out of place in a naturalistic garden. But a good plant marriage shows their casual side. Here, wild columbine mixes well with the rose 'Greuss an Teplitz'.

ABOVE: A block of plants in a single color can serve to frame and draw attention to a prize rosebush. The 'Angel Blush' rose campion, with its small white flowers and gray-green leaves, is clearly a supporting player to the 'Ispahan' rose in this garden.

ABOVE: An occasional unexpected combination can be a hit in the well-planned garden. Roses usually cohabit with common temperate plants, but a gallica rose planted here with Mediterranean euphorbia is a sure winner.

ABOVE: This gardener has gone to great lengths to design a planting that highlights the roses. The strong lines of fountain grass serve as a perfect backdrop for 'The Fairy' rose, while a lamb's ears in the foreground offers contrasting color, shape, and texture.

RIGHT: Roses are true chameleons in the garden. Here, a planting with modest daisies reveals the humble side of roses.

Chapter Four

A ROSE FOR ANY OTHER PLACE

*W*e've all seen the classic rose garden, with row after row of neatly pruned bushes. By virtue of their form and flower—perfected over centuries of breeding—roses can hold their own when planted solo. But if that's the only way you know roses, you don't know what you're missing.

Roses are adaptable. They can crown nearly any type of garden from the formal to the most casual. Perfect border companions, many are well behaved and sophisticated enough for city courtyards. Others will gracefully adorn a suburban porch or a country yard.

Even if your garden is of a more practical nature, don't dismiss the idea of a planting of roses. Herb and vegetable gardens have long been welcome spots for the rose, which is, after all, an herb. No matter what type of garden you have, there's a rose that fits in and lifts it above the ordinary.

OPPOSITE: Aside from color and fragrance, roses contribute their own inimitable form to the border garden. The grandiflora 'Queen Elizabeth' explodes in billows of pink blooms, while white-flowered 'Marie Pavie' presents a more upright, twiggy look. *Rosa multifora* var. *carnea* shows the classic rosebush shape.

RIGHT: Roses form a wall of riotous color that seems to heighten the severe effect of box parterres in this herb garden, making the shades of green seem even more vivid. While we think of the rose as purely ornamental, it is in fact a true herb that has been used medicinally for many centuries.

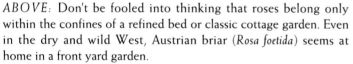

ABOVE: Don't be fooled into thinking that roses belong only within the confines of a refined bed or classic cottage garden. Even in the dry and wild West, Austrian briar (*Rosa foetida*) seems at home in a front yard garden.

ABOVE: Imagine a Texas evening with the sun setting and the fragrant scent of roses wafting over the porch. Porch surrounds are the perfect places to plant roses. They'll hide an unsightly concrete foundation, at the same time providing an inspiring view.

ABOVE: Where architectural lines are straight and materials are simple—such as the adobe and timber of this pueblo-style house—a single rosebush in the courtyard adds color and softens the stark effect. Even in areas with little rainfall, drought- and heat-tolerant roses can be found to ornament the garden.

ABOVE: Roses are quite at home in a formal setting, surrounded by a well-tended lawn and clipped box hedges. The mix of colors found here keeps the planting lively.

RIGHT: A small walled garden seems to be a perfect spot for roses. Ramblers cling to the wall, softening the effect without detracting from the tall spires of foxglove.

LEFT: With their glowing blossoms held high, roses always attract attention. They're dramatic enough to be admired from afar, and can be planted some distance from the house without diminishing their effect.

BELOW: Here, structure is provided by a fountain and sharply edged beds. Luminous white roses spill over the slate edging, adding soft curves to make the garden more welcoming.

ABOVE: A plain garden path can be transformed with the addition of a simple pergola and a few climbing roses. An understory of herbaceous perennials serves to accent the roses 'Botany Bay' and 'Ballerina'.

OPPOSITE: Shrub roses can serve as specimen plants in the landscape. Here, a 'Charles Austin' rosebush boldly stands alone, letting the grace of its flowers claim the attention.

ABOVE: Roses are citizens of the world, at home in any domain. Rambling roses growing against a brick wall exude a rambunctious flair that fits in perfectly with a wild meadow.

LEFT: Roses have a long and storied history in British landscapes. Here, a vibrant pink 'Cockade' rose grows up an arched arbor, offering a focal point in a kitchen garden.

LEFT: With careful selection, roses can serve as landscape high-lights for three seasons of the year. A long-blooming rose, such as this musk, will continue to flower well into autumn, until frost etches its blooms.

BELOW: There may be nothing more enchanting than an exuberant white garden, with blooms tumbling like sea foam, in a formal setting. The roses 'Sombreuil' and 'Pearl Drift' carry off this effect beautifully.

RIGHT: A single rose can have powerful impact when it is trained as a standard. This shining example drifts like a cloud over an underplanting of herbs, including hyssop, thyme, sorrel, and fragrant lavender.

BELOW: Sometimes it's best to just throw caution (and budget) to the wind, and let roses dazzle in their full grandeur. A bold sweep of several varieties along a path is held in place by a yellow-green band of alchemilla.

ABOVE: The country garden requires a thoughtful approach that appears unplanned. Rambling and climbing roses, with their wild flavor, make ideal foundations for such naturalistic plantings.

LEFT: Balance and repetition are important in formal gardens, but that doesn't have to mean a redundancy of plants. Here, a prolific white rose shrub is mirrored by a shapely *Acer* 'Bloodgood' across the path, lending an imaginative harmony to the scene.

ABOVE: In some landscapes, roses are meant to be the main feature. A small, well-mulched bed, carved from a lawn, shows a variety of shrub roses to their best advantage.

OPPOSITE: Clinging to a trellis that mirrors the garden pool, a pair of climbing roses adds a new dimension of color and form to a simple courtyard. Subtle rock garden plants warm the space without detracting from the glory of the roses.